Leo B

The Early Bird

Methuen Drama

Published by Methuen Drama 2006

1 3 5 7 9 10 8 6 4 2

Methuen Drama
A & C Black Publishers Limited
38 Soho Square
London W1D 3HB
www.acblack.com

Copyright © 2006 by Leo Butler

Leo Butler has asserted his rights under the
Copyright, Designs and Patents Act, 1988,
to be identified as the author of this work

ISBN-10: 0 7136 8473 9
ISBN-13: 978 0 7136 8473 5

A CIP catalogue record for this book is available from
the British Library

Typeset by Country Setting, Kingsdown, Kent
Printed and bound in Great Britain by
Bookmarque Ltd, Croydon, Surrey

Caution

This book is produced using paper that is made from wood grown in
managed, sustainable forests. It is natural, renewable and recyclable.
The logging and manufacturing processes conform to the environmental
regulations of the country of origin

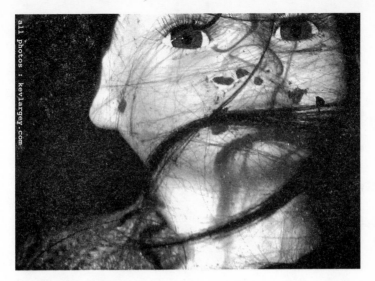

Introduction

I often don't have any grand theme or idea before I start
writing. Sometimes I hear a voice, or I chance upon images
that strike me, and from there just let them guide me on. This
was certainly the case with The Early Bird. The play began
with both the image and voices of a man and a woman, locked
together in an unidentified space, trying to figure out the
reasons why their young daughter has gone missing. From this
starting point I let the drama write itself, discovering the
story as I went along. Only in retrospect can I begin to piece
together my own reasons for writing it, but these reasons are
largely useless for an audience. In fact, I think it would add
little to a production to try and encapsulate the play's
meaning in a couple of digestible sentences. Theatre is alive
and renewed with each performance; the director, the designer
and the actors have brought, and continue to bring, their own
life and interpretation to the text. It is also the job of the
audience to find their own meaning to the play, however
contradictory from mine, and so I prefer to keep my mouth shut.
This is not out of arrogance, but I hope, from a spirit of
respect and sharing.

Leo Butler, '06.

LOTTERY FUNDED

BELFAST FESTIVAL AT QUEEN'S
19th Oct - 4th Nov 2006

RANSOM PRODUCTIONS

Leo Butler (Writer)

MADE OF STONE (Royal Court Upstairs, 2000)

Leo's first play was produced by the Royal court as part of the Young Writers' Festival. "Here is a playwright who already deploys a wide dramatic canvas, Made of Stone is not just a corrosive examination of manhood, it also captures a regional way of living, once bound by heavy industry, manual labour and close, interlocking friendships, now brought to its knees." (Time Out)

REDUNDANT (Royal Court Downstairs, 2001)
Winner George Devine Award for Most Promising Playwright

The court presented Leo's first full-length play in their main stage. In 17 year old Lucy "Butler boldly creates a psychologically complex female lead. He also looks to be a master of stagecraft, subtly manipulating his audience and character with dramatic reversals, before arriving at ending that is inevitable, surprising and loaded with pity and fear" (Evening Standard)

DEVOTION (Theatre Centre tour 2002)

Leo wrote his next play for London's Theatre Centre to tour to secondary schools in England. The play was later revived by TEAM Theatre in Dublin. "While the theme is global (conflict, war, fanaticism) the scale is localizes (three
youngsters on ground wasted by war or urban devastation). Two young lads and a girl play out fantasies of life and love around an abandoned car...There's violence and a sense

of death hovering over all. The audience is left in an
uneasy uncertainty, are we watching children's games or
child combatants? Is it playtime or wartime? Themes of
love, hope and mortality are woven through the action."
(Irish Theatre Magazine)

LUCKY DOG (Royal Court Upstairs, 2004)

Leo's fourth play was staged at the Royal Court, direct-
ed by James Macdonald, and featured Linda Bassett in the
lead role. The play has since been staged in Moscow,
Budapest and Michigan.

"I am still astonished by the 28 year old Butler's
profound understanding of marital solitude.
Nothing much happens on the surface. Yet underneath a
lot goes on as Sue and Eddie, a Sheffield couple in their
late 50s, share a solitary Christmas dinner. Their son
Danny, we learn, is in London with his future bride and
her posh family, but Eddie refuses to answer his calls.
Starved of love by her distracted husband, Sue craves
filial devotion, which she tries to solicit from the
sullen 10 year old next door. Just when you think all
is lost, however, Butler gives you a glimpse of a
future alive with possibilities." (Michael Billington,
The Guardian)

Leo is currently working on commissions for the Royal
National Theatre, the Royal Shakespeare Company and the
Royal Court. Leo's television play Jerusalem The Golden
was broadcast in 2002 on BBC4.

Rachel O'Riordan (Director)

Rachel trained at the Royal Ballet and the Central School Of Speech and Drama and she holds a PhD on Shakespeare from the University of Ulster, and a City and Guilds Senior Award in Theatre Studies. She is Artistic Director of Ransom Productions.

Directing credits include: Everything Is Illuminated (Hampstead Theatre); Miss Julie (Peter Hall Company, Theatre Royal, Bath); Merry Christmas Betty Ford (Lyric, Belfast); The Half (Belfast Festival and The Helix, Dublin); The Man of Mode (Lyric Theatre, Belfast) The Glass Menagerie (Lyric Theatre, Belfast); Tall Tales (Kabosh Theatre; tour); Elizabeth-Almost By Chance a Woman (Kabosh, and Project Theatre, Dublin); Protestants (OMAC, The Traverse Theatre and Soho Theatre, London); 'Tis Pity She's a Whore (Tower Street, Belfast); Hurricane (Soho Theatre; Arts Theatre, West End and E59 off-Broadway); Group (Edinburgh Festival); Cinderella (The Devenish). Rehearsed readings include; Any Other Business (Soho Theatre); Way To Heaven (Queen's Theatre); That Driving Ambition (The Linenhall Theatre) Write Now (Ransom Productions, Belfast Festival) As Associate Director: Sir Peter Hall's Measure for Measure, Theatre Royal, Bath and RSC.

Rachel also has extensive previous experience as a movement director/choreographer. Her credits include Oriana (Project, Dublin); Weddins, Weeins and Wakes, Alice in Wonderland and Hansel and Gretel (Lyric Theatre); Sleep Show and Torch Song Trilogy (Kabosh Theatre).

She has received a number of awards for her work including: 2003 'Best Production' Winner (the Tron Theatre) and 2004 'Best Touring Production' Nominee (Manchester Evening News) for Hurricane; 2004 'Best Production' Nominee (Dublin Theatre Festival) for Elizabeth.

Colm Gormley (Actor)

Previous roles include:
Edgerton in Elizabeth (Kabosh), Astringer in All's Well That
Ends Well (RSC and West End), Richard in Tricky (The Studio,
Richmond), Dessie in Merry Christmas Betty Ford (Lyric,
Belfast), The title role in Woyzeck (Didsbury Studio,
Manchester) Frank in Kvetch (Vienna's English Theatre and the
Edinburgh Fringe), Carl in The Blind bird (Gate Theatre,
London), Demetrius in A Midsummer Night's Dream. Voice One in
Family Voices, Medvedenko in The Seagull, Arturo UI In The
Resistible Rise of Arturo Ui, Flamineo in The White Devil, Sir
Andrew Aguecheek in Twelfth Night, Parris in Romeo and Juliet,
and Aundrey in Three Sister, (all Mercury Theatre, Colchester)
Television includes: Ultimate Force (Bentley Production) and
The Message (BBC)

Abigail McGibbon (Actor)

Abigail graduated from The Gaiety School of Acting, Dublin, in
1992. Her theatre credits include The Gingerbread Mix-Up &
Factory Girls (Bickerstaffe Theatre Co), The Vinegar Fly
(Charabanc), Teechers (Arts Theatre, Belfast), Macbeth(Prime
Cut), Gullivers Travels and Spring Awakening (Galloglass Theatre
Co), Dumped, Convictions & Revenge (Tinderbox), Playboy of the
Western World & The Colleen Bawn (Big Telly Theatre), A
Midsummer Nights Dream, Jane Eyre, Shadowlands, Death of a
Salesman, A Whistle in the Dark, How I Learned t Drive, Hamlet
(a co-production with The Abbey, Dublin) The Glass Menagerie
(Lyric Theatre, Belfast)
Films include H3

Gary McCann (Set Designer)

Gary trained at Nottingham Trent University. His designs for
theatre include "Home by Now" (Baltic Gallery, Newcastle), Top
Girls (Live Theatre, Newcastle),Thieves' Carnival, Jungle Book,
Broken Glass, Arabian Nights (Watermill Theatre, Newbury), The
Glass Menagerie, The Man of Mode, Goblin Market, Merry Christmas
Betty Ford, The Snow Queen, Twelfth Night, Tearing the Loom, The
Visit, Iphigeneia In Aulis (Lyric Theatre, Belfast), The Witch,
The Government Inspector (R.A.D.A), , Elizabeth, Oriana, Romeo
and Juliet (Kabosh Productions, Belfast), Song of the Western
Men, Shang-a-lang,One Snowy Night, and The Lost Child
(Chichester Festival Theatre). His designs for opera include
Promised Land (Marlowe Theatre Canterbury) Les Pecheurs du
Pearls, La Boheme, The Barber of Seville, and La Fille du
Regiment (Swansea City Opera), He also worked as visual artist
on The Quay Thing, a season of ten site-specific performances on
Exeter Quay. He has worked as Art Director and Assistant
Designer on major TV, theatre, and opera productions including
Les Troyens (The Met, New York), Swan Lake (K Ballet, Tokyo),
The Breath of Life, (Haymarket Theatre, London), The Woman in
White (Palace Theatre, London), The Queen of Spades, Sophie's
Choice (Royal Opera House, Covent Garden), Miss World (Channel
5) and The Turner Prize (Channel 4),Gary is Associate Artist
with Ransom Productions. His designs with them include Hurricane
(Soho Theatre/Arts Theatre London, 59th St Theatre New York),
Protestants (Soho Theatre), and The Half (touring).

James Whiteside (Lighting Designer)

James Whiteside graduated from the University of Birmingham in 1999.

Recent lighting design credits include: 'Footloose' and 'Calamity Jane' in the West End and on tour; 'Heroes' at the Churchill, Bromley and on tour; 'Copenhagen' at the Watermill, Newbury; 'Marlon Brando's Corset' at the Yvonne Arnaud, Guildford and on tour; 'Poor Mrs Pepys' at the New Vic, Newcastle-under-Lyme; 'Alice's Adventures In Wonderland' for Chicken Shed Theatre; 'Fen' and 'Five Kinds Of Silence' at Live Theatre, Newcastle; 'Tomfoolery' at the Theatre Royal, Bury St Edmunds and tour; 'Art' at Harrogate Theatre and on tour; 'Dick Barton' at the Croydon Warehouse and 'Destination Anywhere' for Princess Cruises.

For Tall Stories Theatre Company productions include: 'The Gruffalo' in the West End, Off-Broadway and on tour; 'Snow White' Off-Broadway and on tour and 'The Gruffalo's Child' on tour.

Opera includes: 'Maria De Buenos Aires' at Norwich Theatre Royal and on tour; 'HMS Pinafore' for Carl Rosa Opera; 'Madame Butterfly' on a US tour for London City Opera and 'La Traviata' for Surrey Opera.

As Assistant Lighting Designer: 'Mary Stuart', 'Guys And Dolls' and 'Mary Poppins' in the West End. James also revived the lighting for the Donmar's 'Guys And Dolls' and 'This Is How It Goes' on tour and the Royal Opera's 'I Masnadieri' at the Teatro Comunale, Bologna.

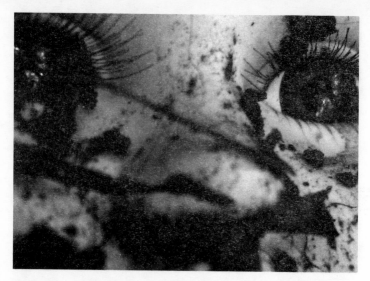

James Kennedy (Sound Designer)

James graduated with a Bsc. Music Technology in 2003 and has been working in theatre since. James has just returned from the Edinburgh Fringe Festival with 'YMT U.K.'s' chamber opera 'Goblin Market'; where he was sound designer and operator. Before this James worked in the 'Lyric Theatre' for over a year as Assistant Technical Stage Manager. In the last year James has toured with Tinderbox theatre company with there production 'Family plot' (sound engineer and SFX designer), has been Technical Stage Manager of Belfast City Council's 'Cultural Diversity Event', Sound Designer and Production manager of Aisling Ghear's 'Diary of a Hunger Striker' and is currently working as Theatre Technician for the University of Ulster Magee Campus.

Russel Allardice (Production Manager)

Russell has worked extensively in theatre and other areas of the entertainment industry. Before moving to Ireland eight years ago, Russell worked as a sound engineer in London's West End and in his native New Zealand. Touring Ireland with Kieran Goss, Patrick Kielty, Guy Clark, Don Williams and Nuala McKeever has been interspersed with periods of venue based technical management at the Burnavon Arts Centre, Cookstown and the Lyric Theatre, Belfast.

Ashley Symth (Deputy Stage Manager)

Since graduating from Queen's University Belfast Ashley has
worked as a freelance stage manager and lighting technician
with many local and touring companies, including Ulster
Theatre Company, Aisling Ghear, Replay, Little Big Top, Class
Acts, Belfast Circus School, Qdos Entertainment, Azido Dance
Ens., NYMT, Production Services Ireland, and Powerlight. She
has also worked on an number of large music events and festivals
as lighting technician and ground rigger. Ashley has toured
extensively with Kabosh Theatre, on "Orianna" (Belfast and tour
of Ireland), "Sleep Show" (Belfast), "Mojo Mickey-bo" (Belfast,
Glasgow, London), "Elizabeth" (Belfast, tour of Ireland, Wales
and England) and "Rhinoceros" (Belfast, Edinburgh Fringe,
London) and with Ransom Productions on "Hurricane" (Belfast,
tour of England , London and Malta), Protestants (Belfast, tour
of Ireland and London) "The Half" (Belfast, tour).

Jorji Wyllie (Assistant Stage Manager)

Jorji has recently graduated with a First in Single Honours Drama
from Queen's University, Belfast. While at university, Jorji was
President of Queen's University Players and coordinated Queen's
entries into the Irish Student Drama Awards (Cork 2006). Her
previous productions include Offending the Audience (Tyrone
Guthrie Society), La Lecon/The Lesson, Yerma (Queen's University
3rd Year production).

COMPANY HISTORY

Ransom Productions was formed in 2002, to produce our first
production, the multi-award winning Hurricane by Richard
Dormer. Hurricane was included in the British Council
Showcase at the Edinburgh Festival 2003 where actor/author
Richard Dormer won the Stage 'Best Actor' Award. The production
was variously described as 'formidable'(The Times) and
'tremendous' (The Telegraph) 'extraordinary (The Independent
*****). Ransom then toured Hurricane to Malta with the British
Council before a UK tour, including the Sheffield Crucible,
before transferring to the Soho Theatre in London for four
weeks. Critical response and audience figures were so exceptional
that the show transferred again, this time to the Arts Theatre,
West End. Hurricane subsequently played for a month off-Broadway, at East59E, again with great success. Hurricane's final run
was at the Grand Opera House, Belfast.   Our next production,
Protestants, was a controversial and dynamic piece of writing by
Robert Welch. Its production at the Old Museum Arts Centre was
the focus of a series of debates, an art exhibition and various
discussion forums. We toured the play to the Traverse,
Edinburgh, where the response to the play was extraordinary
('spine-tinglingly brave', The Scotsman, Edinburgh Evening
News****) We then transferred the show to the Soho; a theatre
Ransom now has established important links with. This production
placed Ransom at the forefront of developmental new writing in
Northern Ireland. Also in 2004 Ransom ran a week-long new
writing workshop, Write Now, culminating in a rehearsed
public reading for four new playwrights. In 2005, Ransom
Productions produced The Half by Richard Dormer; this play was
a huge success at the Belfast festival at Queen's ('..the play
is a runaway success', The Irish Times) and toured to the Helix
in Dublin. Our current production, The Early Bird by Leo Butler,
marks a new development for the company. Butler is a very
established playwright, whose previous plays (Made of Stone,
Redundant, Lucky Dog) have been commissioned and premiered at
the Royal Court Theatre. We are delighted to be working with a
playwright of this calibre.
This Piece of Earth, by Richard Dormer, is in development for
production in 2007. This play is about the Great Hunger, or
Famine, in Ireland in the Nineteenth Century with specific
reference to Northern Ireland. We have also recently
commissioned three new plays for our forthcoming Unspoken
Stories season, which addresses secrets, half-truths and
obfuscation. The three playwrights are; Andrew Muir, Simon Block
and Richard Dormer.
Ransom Productions continues to be an exciting developmental new
writing company. In 2007 we will commence a major three year
project, Write On The Edge, which aims to develop female writers
in Northern Ireland to the point of commission by the company,
production and ultimately transfer to an off-island venue. This
project will link Ransom, and Northern Ireland, to the very best
practitioners, venues and producers.

The Early Bird

Characters

Debbie
Jack

Setting

Feel free to play with the setting and the physicality as pleases you, but do keep the rhythm of the speech.

'La Isla Bonita' is a Madonna song and can be found on *The Immaculate Collection* album.

Long pause.

Debbie   She left for school as normal.

Pause.

Has her breakfast. Coco Pops. Glass of milk.

Pause.

Watch her from the front window. Turns the corner on her way to the bus stop.

Pause.

Must've been what? Twenty past.

Jack   Quarter to.

Debbie   What?

Jack   Quarter to nine.

Debbie   Oh . . .

Jack   She was late.

Debbie   I was running late.

Jack   Right.

Debbie   The clock's gone forward. I forgot to set the . . . the . . .

Pause.

The thing.

Jack   What?

Debbie   I forgot to set the . . .

Pause.

Only realise once I turn on the news. Of course there was no news. Not at that time. What's the one?

Jack   What?

Debbie   What's it called? You know the one, what is it?

Jack   What?

Debbie   The programme. Straight after the news.

Jack   I wouldn't know.

Debbie   You'd left already.

Pause.

You'd left already.

Jack   I was in a rush.

Debbie   You had an early start, that's right. That's what I thought, anyway. 'He's got off early,' I thought. 'Someone's got the wind in his sails.'

Jack   You weren't thinking.

Debbie   No.

Jack   You were carrying on as normal.

Debbie   She has her breakfast, I turn on the news.

Pause.

Jack   What's she wearing?

Pause.

Debbie *and* **Jack**   What's she wearing?

Pause.

Jack   Debbie . . .

Debbie   'Bargain Hunt'.

Jack   What?

Debbie   The programme. 'Bargain Hunt', I remember now. She's got on her little orange mac. With the hood pulled up. Turns the corner and goes to catch the bus. 'Course all the other kids have left by now. I gave her a note to pass on to her teacher. I was going to ring, but . . . but I was late myself, I wasn't . . .

Pause.

You don't think, do you?

Pause.

You don't think anything's going to happen.

Jack She'd been restless.

Debbie What?

Jack Come to think of it. Thinking back.

Pause.

She hadn't been herself.

Debbie I wouldn't say that.

Pause.

I wouldn't.

Pause.

No different to any girl her age. Growing up. That age.

Jack You think it's all part of . . .

Debbie Growing up, that's what I said.

Jack You think.

Debbie What?

Jack *You* think.

Pause.

Debbie Jack. My partner, Jack. He thought she'd been restless.

Jack It's the little things you notice.

Debbie He says that now.

Jack The little things.

Debbie You say that now.

Jack   She's put on weight.

Debbie   You see.

Jack   She can barely fit into her own clothes.

Debbie   Oh . . .

Jack   The junk you feed her. Mars bars and fucking Monster Munch.

Debbie   So it's my fault?

Pause.

Jack   She was distant.

Debbie   Oh . . .

Jack   Reclusive.

Debbie   Come on, Jack . . .

Jack   She was.

Debbie   Like any girl that age. Growing up.

Long pause.

Of course, it'd be different had she been a boy. Maybe she would have been more . . .

Jack   Outgoing.

Debbie   Maybe.

Jack   Maybe so.

Debbie   With you at least.

Pause.

With her father.

Jack   Fine.

Debbie   With him.

Long pause.

What we're saying . . .

Pause.

What we're trying to say . . .

Jack   Maybe there was and maybe there wasn't.

Debbie   It wasn't . . .

Jack   Something.

Debbie   . . . anything either of us had really . . .

Jack   Something else going on.

Debbie   She would have told us.

Pause.

She would have told me at least.

Jack   You can't help but think the worst.

Debbie   She hadn't been picked on or anything.

Jack   We don't know that.

Debbie   She kept herself to herself.

Jack   We can't be sure of anything now.

Debbie   She's a good girl.

Jack   Right.

Debbie   An angel.

Long pause.

Jack   Debbie.

Pause.

Debbie . . .

Debbie   At least she never said.

Jack   Should I go and check on her?

Debbie   At least.

Pause.

At least she never said anything to my face.

Jack   Debbie . . .

Debbie   You don't just disappear.

Jack   Should I see that she's all right?

Debbie   You don't vanish into thin air.

Pause.

Well, do you?

Jack   No.

Debbie   Well, do you, Jack?

Long pause.

She wakes up the following morning and . . .

Jack   I'm running late.

Debbie   Have you seen her gym bag?

Jack   Debbie, please . . .

Debbie   I left it by the settee last night.

Jack   I haven't seen it.

Debbie   Are you sure you didn't move it?

Jack   Debbie . . .

Debbie   You were the last one to bed.

Jack   For Christ's sake, will you get out of my way?

Debbie   She's going to be late already.

Jack   I didn't even know she had a fucking gym bag!

Debbie   Jack . . .

Jack   Gym bag.

Debbie   Jack, don't . . .

Jack   How many bags does she need, for fucksake?

Debbie Don't swear in front of her.

Jack Jesus Christ . . .

Debbie Don't swear, I said!

Jack I don't have time for this, Deborah.

Debbie Frighten the poor girl.

Jack Will you . . . ?

Debbie She's hardly touched her Coco Pops, look.

Jack Oh now . . .

Debbie Look at her.

Jack Will you let me get my coat at least?

Debbie Jack . . .

Jack Stood there like the fucking Andes.

Debbie Don't . . .

Jack The pair of you.

Debbie Don't speak to me like that.

Jack Have you seen the time already?!

Debbie Jack . . .

Jack Fucking useless, what are you?!

Pause.

Well?!

Pause.

Fucking useless.

Debbie The thing.

Jack What?

Debbie The thing, I forgot to set the . . .

Pause.

The . . .

Pause.

The thing, the . . .

Pause.

The programme, straight after the news. I remember because I changed the channel, I changed the channel. We have a box now, don't we?

Jack   We do.

Debbie   There's what, about a hundred fucking channels on the thing?

Jack   Right.

Debbie   I mean, it's mostly old crap, we don't . . .

Jack   Repeats.

Debbie   We don't really . . .

Jack   We don't really care for it too much.

Debbie   He likes the sport.

Jack   Sky Sports. For the cricket.

Debbie   Sorry, I don't mean to swear, I . . .

Jack   The test match.

Debbie   I don't normally . . .

Jack   The Ashes.

Debbie   It's not something I normally do. Not while she's . . .

Jack   Though I can't say I'm too fussy, you know? Boxing, the footy, golf. The beach fucking volleyball – if you get my meaning, boys.

Debbie   She's on her way out the door, and I go to call for her – I mean, she's worse than I am for forgetting what she . . .

Pause.

I'm late myself, but . . .

Pause.

But, you know?

Pause.

It can just suck you in though, can't it? The channels, I mean.

Pause.

They suck you in.

Long pause.

'Bargain Hunt'.

Pause.

'Doctors'.

Pause.

'A Place in the Sun'.

Pause.

'A Place in the Sun'.

Jack   Debbie . . .

Debbie   You remember?

Jack   Look . . .

Debbie   You remember, Jack?

Pause. She sings the chorus of 'La Isla Bonita', pausing between the first four lines and the second four lines.

Long pause.

Jack   You should call her friends.

Debbie   What?

Jack   Her friends.

Pause.

You should see if anyone's seen her.

Debbie   I don't have their numbers.

Jack   Have you checked upstairs?

Debbie   I don't . . .

Jack   Have you checked her room?

Pause.

Deborah.

Pause.

Have you looked through her drawer?

Pause.

Her things.

Debbie   What things?

Jack   Perhaps she kept a diary. Most girls her age . . .

Pause.

Check her drawer.

Debbie   No.

Jack   She might have left something.

Debbie   No, I'm thinking.

Jack   A clue, she might've written something down in her schoolwork.

Debbie   No, it wasn't. It wasn't raining, I mean. Not first thing anyway. She must've worn her blazer. Her blazer and her scarf – that's right.

Jack   Debbie . . .

Debbie   That's right. She took her blazer and her scarf, and I told her to take her umbrella.

Jack   Should I go and look for it myself?

Pause.

Debbie.

Pause.

Debbie.

Long pause.

Are you going to just fucking sit there?!

Long pause.

Debbie   Of course he's quite the temper on him.

Jack   Debbie, please . . .

Debbie   Not that you'd know it, just to look at him.

Jack   We can't . . .

Debbie   Quite the temper.

Jack   All right . . .

Debbie   Quite the man.

Jack   All right, that's . . .

Debbie   Quite the man about town.

Pause.

Not that you'd ever suspect, of course.

Jack   Deborah . . .

Debbie   Not from him, oh no.

Jack   Look . . .

Debbie   It's not in his nature.

Jack   Turn it off.

Debbie   Not with all he's achieved.

Jack   Give me the remote.

Debbie   And at such a young age.

Jack   We'll never get any sleep if you carry on . . .

Debbie   Coming home from work with his angel all gone.

Jack   She's not sleeping, Debbie.

Debbie   His angel all gone.

Long pause.

Jack   I should call them myself.

Debbie   He says.

Jack   She must have kept a diary. Most girls her age . . .

Pause.

Debbie   What?

Jack   What?

Debbie   Most girls what?

Long pause.

Jack   There must be something, there must be . . .

Pause.

Something, some . . .

Debbie   A clue.

Jack   Right.

Debbie   Something she was keeping from you.

Jack   From us.

Debbie   Some secret you made her promise . . .

Jack   Debbie, please . . .

Debbie   Something you made her . . . .

Jack   Will you let me get my coat at least?

Debbie   Jack . . .

Jack   Stood there like the fucking Andes.

Debbie Don't . . .

Jack The pair of you.

Debbie Don't speak to me like that.

Jack Have you seen the time already?!

Debbie Jack . . .

Jack Fucking useless, what are you?!

Pause.

Well?!

Pause.

Fucking useless.

Debbie Come on now, girl, let's have you on your way.

Jack I swear to God you do it on purpose.

Debbie Let's put your little coat on now.

Jack Debbie . . .

Debbie Pull your hood up.

Jack Don't ignore me!

Debbie Yes, I know you don't want to, but . . .

Jack Debbie!

Debbie You're going to get yourself soaked.

Jack Did you do it on purpose?

Debbie Please, Kimberly, don't . . .

Jack Answer me!

Debbie That's it, and your umbrella now.

Jack If you don't give me a straight answer . . .

Debbie Hold it.

Jack Debbie . . .

Debbie   Hold it. Like this. Hold the umbrella like this. In your hand.

Jack   It's not raining.

Debbie   The weatherman said . . .

Jack   The weatherman.

Debbie   The weatherman said it's going to rain today.

Jack   You'll believe anything.

Debbie   She's going to get herself soaked like this, now . . .

Jack   Let her go.

Debbie   Kimberly.

Jack   If she doesn't want to . . .

Debbie   Look at me.

Jack   You can't . . .

Debbie   Turn around.

Jack   Jesus Christ . . .

Debbie   Tell her.

Jack   What?

Debbie   Listen to your father.

Jack   It's late enough already.

Debbie   Tell her.

Jack   Leave the girl alone.

Debbie   Tell her.

Jack   I don't have . . .

Debbie   Tell her, Jack!

Long pause.

I told you to take the umbrella.

Pause.

Kimberly.

Jack No.

Debbie What?

Pause.

What did you just say?

Pause.

Just in case now, come on.

Jack I don't want to.

Debbie Oh . . .

Jack I don't want to.

Debbie Now you're just being . . .

Jack Don't make me, Mammy, please.

Debbie Put it in your bag at least.

Jack But . . .

Debbie Give me your bag.

Jack No, please . . .

Debbie It hardly weighs a thing now, come on.

Pause.

Come on, come here.

Pause.

What have I told you?

Pause.

Hm?

Pause.

The early bird catches what?

Pause.

What does he catch? – Don't look at the floor.

Pause.

The early bird catches what?

Jack   The worm.

Debbie   What?

Jack   The worm.

Debbie   The what worm?

Jack   The wiggly.

Debbie   The wiggly what?

Pause.

The wiggly what now?

Beat.

The wiggly what?

Jack *giggles.*

Debbie   Come on, you just said so – The wiggly . . . ?

Jack (*giggles*)   No, don't . . .

Debbie   The wiggly . . .

Jack (*giggles*)   The wiggly worm.

Debbie   What?

Jack (*giggles*)   Please . . .

Debbie   I can't hear you.

Jack (*laughing*)   Stop!

Debbie   I can't hear . . .

Jack (*laughing*)   Don't tickle me, please!

Debbie   The wiggly what?

Jack (*laughing*)   The worm, the wiggly worm!

Debbie (*laughing*)   Who's a wiggly?

Jack (*laughing*)   Mammy, please!

Debbie (*laughing*)   Who's a wiggly worm?

Jack (*laughing*)   Stop it, please!!

Both laughing.

Pause.

Debbie   Go on now, there's a good girl.

Pause.

You don't want to disappoint Mrs Stephens.

Pause.

Kimberly.

Pause.

You don't want to upset your father now, do you?

Pause.

Well?

Pause.

You don't want to upset anyone.

Pause.

Kimberly.

Pause.

Kimberly, please . . .

Jack   Take your clothes off.

Debbie   Kimberly . . .

Jack   Take your clothes off, come on.

Pause.

It's freezing cold, come to bed.

Pause.

Come on now, Kimberly love, it's way past your bedtime.

Debbie   But . . .

Jack   No buts, come on.

Debbie   But Daddy . . .

Jack   Daddy nothing – bed.

Debbie   But I'm not tired, Daddy.

Jack   You've got a big day ahead of you tomorrow, now come on, snuggle up, there's a good girl.

Debbie   Sleepy.

Jack   What?

Debbie   I'm not sleepy.

Jack   Of course you're sleepy, you're a sleepy-socks, we all know that.

Debbie   Daddy, please . . .

Jack   You're fighting the sleep because you're excited.

Debbie   No.

Jack   You're nervous about the big day, poor thing.

Debbie   But I'm . . .

Jack   Pull the covers up, there's a good girl.

Debbie   Can I keep the light on?

Jack   You can have anything you want, my love, you know that.

Debbie   Can I sleep in your room?

Jack   No.

Debbie   Oh . . .

Jack   I might read you a story, if you'd like.

Pause.

Would you like that?

Debbie   Yes, Daddy.

Jack   You'd like that, wouldn't you?

Debbie   Yes . . .

Jack   So long as you're good now. So long as you stay in bed and stop bothering your mammy and me.

Debbie   But . . .

Jack   No more noise.

Debbie   I heard shouting.

Jack   That's just the television. Your mammy's TV.

Debbie   Oh . . .

Jack   You shouldn't let that bother you – now, go to sleep.

Debbie   But I heard you . . .

Jack   Go to sleep.

Debbie   Daddy, please . . .

Jack   You were having nightmares, that's all.

Pause.

Tell the truth now.

Debbie   But . . .

Jack   You were having nightmares and they woke you up.

Pause.

Tell the truth now.

Debbie   I'll try, Daddy.

Jack   The monsters.

Debbie Yes . . .

Jack The grizzly old monsters with their eyes bursting out their heads. They were climbing up the wall outside, weren't they?

Pause.

Kimberly . . .

Debbie Yes . . .

Jack They were tapping at the window.

Debbie They were, Daddy, yes.

Jack They were scraping their nails against the glass and you could see their faces behind the curtains.

Pause.

Well, couldn't you?

Pause.

Kimberly . . .

Debbie Daddy, please . . .

Jack You could see them, couldn't you?

Debbie But . . .

Jack You could smell them.

Debbie Yes, Daddy.

Jack There's small wonder you can't sleep. Little darling, scared to death.

Debbie I think I saw them.

Jack You think.

Debbie I think . . .

Jack They're only nightmares, come on.

Pause.

They're bad dreams.

Debbie   But I . . .

Jack   There's no one coming to get you.

Debbie   I heard you.

Jack   There's no such thing as monsters.

Debbie   But . . .

Jack   There's no such thing as monsters.

Long pause.

Would you like the story about Jesus?

Pause.

Kimberly.

Pause.

Jesus kills all the monsters. You know that, don't you?

Long pause.

What story would you like?

Pause.

Kimberly.

Pause.

Kimberly, love . . .

Debbie   Of course, the nights are getting darker.

Jack   This is true.

Debbie   You lose an hour.

Jack   Lost.

Debbie   What?

Jack   Just like that.

Pause.

Away with the fairies.

Debbie   The days and nights are getting darker.

Jack   Right.

Debbie   She turns the corner of the street to the bus stop. She turns the corner of the street, I change the channels. Though I'm only watching with half an eye, mind. She joins her friends at the bus stop. There's Peggy and little Rachel. And there's Richard, look. They're calling over to her as she dashes across the street. She has her umbrella now . . .

Jack   She's not alone.

Debbie   No, they're jealous.

Jack   They're her friends.

Debbie   They're her jealous friends.

Pause.

Jealous bastards.

Pause.

Fucking animals.

Long pause.

Jack . . .

Jack   She has her umbrella and she joins them under the shelter.

Pause.

She has her umbrella and she . . .

Debbie   No, she's alone, you're right.

Pause.

She's frightened.

Pause.

She's frightened of the dark.

Pause.

She's an angel.

Pause.

She's lit up like a beacon in the dark. She's got on her little orange mac with the hood pulled up.

Pause.

She's got on her blazer and her scarf, and I . . .

Pause.

She's with her friends.

Pause.

No.

Pause.

No, she . . .

Jack   Perhaps she's with them now.

Pause.

Her friends.

Debbie   Who?

Jack   Her good friends.

Debbie   Fucking animals.

Jack   Oh, come on, Deborah . . .

Debbie   The dirty beasts.

Jack   She's the one . . .

Debbie   She's an angel.

Jack   The junk you feed her, there's little wonder . . .

Debbie   I don't have their numbers, I told you.

Jack   Debbie . . .

Debbie   I don't.

Long pause.

She turns the corner and meets them. Her good, kind friends. Of course she's not alone. We're not the only ones to forget the . . .

Pause.

The thing, the . . .

Jack   The event itself is not unusual.

Debbie   Thank you, she's not – We're not, I mean . . . My partner and I.

Jack   It's an easy mistake to make.

Debbie   If there was any reason to believe . . .

Jack   To believe.

Debbie   Otherwise, I mean.

Jack   If we thought for any reason . . .

Debbie   She loves us.

Pause.

She loves us both so much. From the bottom of her tiny heart.

Pause.

We brought her into this world.

Pause.

We brought her in, Jack.

Long pause.

As before, she sings the chorus of 'La Isla Bonita'. **Jack** *joins in singing the last two lines.*

Long pause.

Debbie   Jack.

Pause.

Jack . . .

Jack   I mean, it's not as if we had any . . .

Debbie   Suspicions.

Jack   It's not like we had any doubts . . .

Debbie   We weren't concerned with . . .

Jack   Apart from.

Debbie   Yes.

Jack   The little things.

Debbie   So you say.

Jack   The little things you notice.

Pause.

Habits.

Pause.

Habits.

Debbie   I heard you the first time.

Jack   She's a dreamer.

Debbie   So?

Jack   From the moment they pulled her head out.

Debbie   What?

Jack   They pulled her head out with the forceps and she was never the same since.

Debbie   She . . . ?

Jack   Even the doctor said so.

Debbie   Which doctor?

Jack   The anaesthetist.

Debbie   Who?

Jack   The doctor.

Debbie I . . .

Jack She doesn't remember.

Debbie I don't . . .

Jack She's fucking out of it, boys, I tell you.

Debbie Which doctor?

Jack They clamped her head with the forceps . . .

Debbie Jack . . .

Jack They cut you.

Pause.

They cut you . . .

Debbie No, you're right.

Jack I know I'm right.

Debbie She was free.

Jack What?

Debbie Free.

Jack They spread her out on the table and they cut you.

Debbie She was free, Jack.

Jack From your hole.

Long pause.

They spread her out on the table . . .

Debbie Shaking her little fists.

Jack The head on it.

Debbie Poor darling.

Jack The head . . .

Debbie Her poor misshapen head.

Jack Special needs.

Debbie   What?

Jack   Abnormal.

Debbie   Oh . . .

Jack   The junk you feed it.

Debbie   Oh, she's special all right.

Jack   From your gash.

Debbie   Jack . . .

Jack   Keep it in your knickers, woman.

Long pause.

Of course you don't notice anything until . . .

Debbie   Until it's over.

Pause.

It's not over.

Pause.

It's over.

Jack   Debbie . . .

Debbie   It's over.

Jack   Look . . .

Debbie   It's over – listen to her, Jack!

Jack   Debbie, please . . .

Debbie   I can't stand it any more, I can't . . .

Jack   She's just tired.

Debbie   I can't do this.

Jack   Pay no attention . . .

Debbie   Stuck in this house all day . . .

Jack   You're just . . .

Debbie   Stuck with this . . . .

Jack   You're not thinking straight.

Debbie   This fucking / thing! . . .

Jack   Even the doctor said so.

Debbie   Listen to her, Jack!

Jack   Most babies . . .

Debbie   I wish she'd just / vanish! . . .

Jack   Most babies cry through the night.

Debbie   Stuck on my breast . . .

Jack   Your tit.

Debbie   Draining the very life like some . . .

Jack   Hand her over.

Debbie   Bitch.

Jack   Debbie . . .

Debbie   Deformed little bitch.

Jack   Debbie, please . . .

Debbie   I hope you choke on it.

Pause.

Did I say that out loud?

Pause.

Oh, poor mite.

Jack   Hand her over.

Pause.

Debbie . . .

Debbie   You're doing it on purpose.

Jack   Let me help you.

Debbie   If only to shut her up.

Jack   You're not . . .

Debbie   If only for a moment's peace.

Jack   You can't keep . . .

Debbie   The neighbours, Jack!

Jack   Who?

Debbie   Think of the neighbours.

Jack   Fuck the neighbours.

Debbie   What will they think?

Jack   Most babies . . .

Debbie   What will they think?

Jack   They make an effort, Debbie.

Debbie   Do they?

Jack   They make themselves heard, it's only natural.

Pause.

Come on now, let's . . .

Debbie   Of course we're fine.

Jack   What?

Debbie   We're fine, aren't we, Jack?

Jack   They say it's common.

Debbie   Right.

Jack   The first three months are always hard . . .

Debbie   But after that.

Jack   After that, yes.

Debbie   You should pop over for lunch one day.

Jack   Oh, definitely.

Debbie   Sunday lunch.

Jack   She'd love to meet you.

Debbie   I'll be back at work soon.

Jack   I mean, she's not really . . .

Debbie   Childcare.

Jack   She's not exactly . . .

Debbie   I mean, we don't feel any different, do we?

Jack   No.

Debbie   We're still the same old . . .

Jack   Same old.

Debbie   It's not like you have to stop coming to visit.

Jack   An extra pair of hands, that's all.

Debbie   She's adorable.

Jack   She'll be in her own room soon.

Debbie   You will come and visit us, won't you?

Long pause.

Jack   Debbie . . .

Debbie   I suppose had she been a boy.

Jack   What?

Debbie   Had she been a boy with golden hair. Had she taken after her father. Had she been more . . .

Jack   Had she shown some interest, at least.

Debbie   Had she . . .

Jack   The junk you feed her.

Debbie   Had she been a boy.

Jack   Mars bars and fucking Monster Munch.

Debbie   So it's my fault?

Jack   You should smell that toilet after she's used it for Christ knows what.

Debbie   Her grades, Jack.

Jack   What?

Debbie   Her grades. She has good grades.

Jack   She has average grades.

Debbie   I mean, she's no prodigy.

Jack   Average.

Debbie   She's no freak of fucking nature.

Jack   She's an average student.

Debbie   For her age.

Jack   For any age.

Debbie   She's the youngest in her year.

Jack   She can barely fit into her . . . .

Debbie   Jack. My partner, Jack. He thinks she's retarded.

Jack   The junk you feed her.

Debbie   He thinks.

Jack   Mars bars and fucking Monster Munch.

Debbie   Small wonder they're so jealous. She's with her friends at the bus stop. Of course they're jealous of her grades . . .

Jack   Her average grades.

Debbie   They're talking and laughing and whispering in one another's ears.

Jack   They're pushing each other around.

Debbie   Her friends.

Jack   They're of that age.

Debbie   There's Peggy and Rachel and Richard, and they call to her from the shelter.

Jack   'It's gone half past, Kim!'

Debbie   They're going to be in so much trouble.

Jack   'Kimberly!'

Debbie   Peggy, Rachel and Richard . . .

Jack   'Come on now, hurry!'

Debbie   They're going to get drenched.

Jack   'Get a move on, will you?!'

Debbie   Drenched.

Jack   'Stupid fat cow!'

Debbie   She's got her umbrella and she's so popular now.

Jack   For an average girl.

Debbie   They're so jealous and she's so popular and they're whispering in one another's ears.

Jack   They're whispering about her.

Debbie   No, they . . .

Jack   They're whispering about her.

Debbie   Jack . . .

Jack   I mean, who can fucking blame them, eh?

Debbie   You've left already.

Jack   I . . .

Debbie   You've gone, Jack.

Pause.

You've gone.

Jack   Fine.

Debbie I change the channels and they're going to be in so much trouble by the time they actually get there. She opens up her brolly and the four of them huddle up. The rain's beating down around them . . .

Jack What's the time?

Debbie They don't care what time it is, they're . . .

Jack 'Stupid fat cow, look at her.'

Debbie 'Remedial.'

Jack 'Waddling like a penguin.'

Debbie 'Take her bag.'

Jack 'What?'

Debbie 'Take her bag, Richard, go on.'

Jack 'Wipe my bum with it, you mean?'

Debbie 'Throw it into the road.'

Jack 'Oh . . . '

Debbie 'Throw it under the bus.'

Jack 'Throw her under the bus.'

Debbie 'Stupid fat cow.'

Jack 'Blubber mountain, can't put two sentences together.'

Debbie 'Give me the scissors.'

Jack 'What?'

Debbie 'Ask Mrs Stephens for the scissors, go on.'

Jack 'Cut her hair off?'

Debbie 'Cut her fat off.'

Jack 'You're cruel.'

Debbie 'Puncture her belly.'

Jack 'Her head.'

Debbie   'Cut open her hole, snip snip snip.'

Jack   'Snip, snip, snip!'

Debbie   'Take her piggy eyes out, go on!'

Jack   Who can blame them, eh?

Debbie   Turn it up, Jack, please!

Long pause.

'Richard and Judy'.

Pause.

Jack   Debbie . . .

Debbie   'Friends'.

Pause.

'America's Next Top . . . . '

Jack   What's she wearing?

Long pause.

Debbie *and* **Jack**   What's she wearing?

Pause.

Jack   Debbie . . .

Debbie   I forgot the . . .

Jack   What?

Debbie   I forgot the thing, the . . .

Pause.

I forgot to set the . . .

Long pause.

Of course the bus doesn't come.

Pause.

The driver, the bus driver. He forgets.

Jack   Right.

Debbie   He forgot to set the . . .

Pause.

The thing, the . . .

Jack   Have you called them?

Debbie   The thing, he forgets to set the . . .

Jack   Are you going to just fucking sit there?!

Long pause.

She turns the corner . . .

Pause.

She was late, I was running late.

Pause.

You were carrying on as normal.

Pause.

Debbie . . .

Debbie   'Someone's got the wind in his sails.'

Jack   What?

Debbie   That's what I thought. 'Someone's in an awful hurry this morning.'

Pause.

'Someone's got the itch.'

Jack   Now, look . . .

Debbie   'Where's he off to so early?' I thought.

Jack   Let's not get carried away.

Debbie   'With a twinkle in his eye.'

Jack   Oh, come on . . .

Debbie   With a twinkle in your eye.

Pause.

With a twinkle . . .

Jack   She was late, I was running late.

Debbie   Dirty slut.

Jack   I get up at the same time every morning. I go to the bathroom, have a wash, brush my teeth. I return via the landing to the bedroom and I take my clothes that are laying neatly on the top of the chest of drawers. Of course, I used to wear a suit to work when I was just an apprentice, back in the day. Back in the day, Christ, I must have got over two dozen suits locked away in that fucking wardrobe of mine. I mean, they're good suits, give or take, I think they're partly responsible for getting me to where I am today, fucking shallow bastard management. Though now I'm virtually running the place, well, I can wear whatever I fucking feel like, can't I? I could go dressed as King fucking Kong for all they fucking care.

Debbie   Does she whisper in your ear?

Jack   What?

Debbie   Does she call out your name, Jack?

Jack   Though I still take pride in my appearance, don't get me wrong.

Debbie   Jack . . .

Jack   I have it ironed and folded on the top of the chest of drawers by eight o'clock each night. It only takes me about ten minutes to be up and ready to leave by the time that fucking alarm clock goes off, so I go to the bathroom, have a wash . . .

Debbie   Does she ask about me?

Jack   Look . . .

Debbie   Does she even know?

Pause.

Jack . . .

Jack   I go to the bathroom, have a wash – I'm out the fucking door by half past eight. I'm out the door and I'm behind the wheel and the sun's beating down through the windscreen. Of course, on a good day I might pop into the gym for an hour, this is only on a good day mind, if there's no poor bastard waiting to get sacked or some gobshite from IT needs to reinstall the fucking hard drive for the third time in two months – then I might consider it, right? Twenty minutes on the cross-trainer, a few weights – work up the abdominals, you know? I mean, a man's got to keep his figure, hasn't he? A man's got to make the most of what he's got. You don't get to where I am looking like a fucking Neanderthal, d'you know what I mean? You have to stay positive, right? You have to think positive, you have to . . .

Debbie   Does she whisper sweet nothings?

Jack   You have to think positive, Debbie.

Pause.

Go to the gym.

Pause.

Fold the clothes and place them on top of the chest of drawers.

Pause.

Debbie.

Pause.

Fold and place them on . . .

Debbie   She shuts the door behind her and turns the corner at the end of street. Of course, there was no news at that time.

Jack   Of course.

Debbie   There wasn't any . . .

Jack   I mean, don't get me wrong, it's not like I haven't been there, you know? It's not as if I don't . . .

Debbie   At the start.

Jack   At the start, that's right.

Pause.

Watching her grow.

Pause.

The first time she smiled.

Pause.

The first time she called me by my name.

Pause.

Dressing her up. Her little pink outfits.

Debbie   Her dresses.

Jack   Her socks and little mittens.

Debbie   Her sweet winter hat.

Jack   Dressed up and out to meet her friends.

Debbie   All her little parties.

Jack   And everyone pawing over her . . .

Debbie   The neighbours.

Jack   Everyone . . .

Debbie   Next door.

Jack   Her fucking grandparents.

Debbie   The neighbours, Jack.

Jack   In her little winter bonnet . . .

Debbie   What will they think?

Pause.

Biting at my nipple . . .

Jack   Hand her over.

Debbie   Draining the very . . .

Jack   Debbie.

Debbie   If only she would / vanish!

Jack   Go back to sleep, will you?!

Long pause.

You were carrying on as normal.

Debbie   Coco Pops. Glass of milk.

Jack   You weren't thinking.

Debbie   An angel.

Jack   What?

Debbie   She turns the corner like an angel and her friends are waiting for her. They're calling over to her, but I forgot to . . .

Jack   Fold and place them on the top of the chest of drawers, that's right. A man needs his routine, Deborah, you can't blame me for that. A man needs reason, there has to be reason to get out of that fucking bed every morning, you have to think positive – the pair of you, fucking bad as each other . . .

Debbie   The thing, the . . .

Jack   We must have reason, Debbie.

Pause.

We must have reason.

Long pause.

She left for school as normal.

Pause.

She has her breakfast . . .

Debbie   'Bargain Hunt'.

Jack   What?

Debbie   'Bargain Hunt', the programme.

Pause.

The programme . . .

Jack   I wouldn't know.

Debbie   You'd left already.

Jack   Right.

Debbie   'Richard and Judy'.

Pause.

'Friends'.

Pause.

'America's Next Top Model'.

Pause.

'Dad's Army'.

Pause.

'Neighbours'.

Pause.

'The Weakest Link'.

Pause.

'The Simpsons'.

Pause.

'EastEnders', now I like this one. We like this one, don't we, Jack? We like something with a good story.

Pause.

'The Nazis and the Final Solution'.

Pause.

'Celebrity Love Island'.

Pause.

'Newsnight'.

Pause.

'Newsnight'.

Jack   Turn it off, would you?

Debbie   What?

Jack   Go to sleep.

Debbie   Of course, there was no news . . .

Jack   That's enough.

Pause.

Debbie   MTV.

Pause.

The fucking state of that one, look.

Jack   Eminem.

Debbie   Who?

Pause.

Who?

Jack   Blondie bollocks.

Debbie   Oh . . .

Jack   Turn it off, I said.

Debbie   What?

Jack   Turn it off.

Pause.

Well, go on.

Pause.

Go on.

Debbie   It's an old one, look, Jack.

Pause.

Jack, look.

Jack   Right.

Debbie   You know, I haven't seen this one in years. – What's their name again?

Pause.

Their name, what's their – ? You know the name.

Jack   The Marx Brothers.

Debbie   Who?

Jack   Groucho, Harpo and Chico.

Debbie   What channel is this?

Jack   TCM.

Debbie   Turn it up.

Jack   'Animal Crackers'.

Debbie   What?

Jack   The name of the movie. 'Animal Crackers'.

Debbie   But I can't hear anything.

Jack   You should try and get some sleep.

Debbie   Where is it?

Pause.

Where is it, Jack?

Jack   What?

Debbie   The remote.

Jack   I don't . . .

Debbie   You've hidden the remote.

Jack   I don't have the fucking . . .

Debbie   You're lying on it.

Jack   For Christ's sake . . .

Debbie   Jack!

Jack   Keep your voice down, would you?

Debbie   Pull the cover up.

Jack   What?

Debbie   The quilt.

Jack   You're going to wake her . . .

Debbie   Pull the quilt over your head . . .

Jack   Debbie . . .

Debbie   The quilt, you murdering cunt!

Long pause.

Jack   Debbie . . .

Debbie   Quiet.

Jack   Do you hear?

Pause.

I swear I can hear her, listen.

Long pause.

I can hear her – Debbie.

Pause.

Do you not hear her?

Long pause.

Should I go to see if she's all right?

Pause.

Debbie . . .

Debbie   I'm watching.

Jack   She's got school in a few hours.

Debbie   Then you should have thought of that before.

Jack   What?

Pause.

I should have thought of what before?

Pause.

I should have thought . . . ?

Debbie   Dirty slut.

Pause.

The dirty, filthy slut.

Long pause.

I expect she's blonde.

Pause.

Her blonde hair tumbling over his desk and into the open drawers.

Pause.

Young.

Pause.

Young and free.

Pause.

She's captain of the volleyball team.

Pause.

Has she been cut?

Pause.

Did they cut her open too, Jack?

Jack   Take your clothes off.

Debbie   Right.

Jack   Take your clothes off.

Debbie   That's right.

Jack   Come on.

Debbie   That's perfect.

Jack   You'll catch your death of cold now, get under the covers.

Debbie   And which way would you like it, sir?

Pause.

Would you like to enter from behind?

Jack   Well . . .

Debbie   Might I bend over for you?

Jack   If you like.

Debbie   He says.

Jack   I'd like that, yes.

Debbie   Locking the door.

Jack   That would be very decent of you, Jenny.

Debbie   Her blonde hair tumbling . . .

Jack   You know a man must take care of his physique.

Debbie   Slowly pulling down her knickers.

Jack   Yes, sir.

Debbie   She says.

Jack   Of course, sir.

Debbie   She says.

Jack   Of course.

Debbie   Of course she hasn't been cut, oh no.

Jack   Let me bend over your desk, sir.

Debbie   Her tight neat gash, with her tongue round his pole. Her blonde hair tumbling . . .

Jack   Let me bend over for you.

Debbie   You can tell I've been working out.

Jack   Oh yes, sir.

Debbie   You can feel my biceps.

Jack   Yes . . .

Debbie   Feel my biceps, Jenny.

Jack   Is that better, sir?

Debbie   Deeper.

Jack   It's not too tight for you, I hope.

Debbie   Deeper, come on.

Jack   It's not too tight for you.

Debbie   Her blonde hair tumbling . . .

Jack   It's not too much for you . . .

Debbie   What?

Jack   It's not too . . .

Debbie   What did you just say? It's not too what?

Jack   It's . . . .

Debbie   Not too what-now?

Jack *giggles.*

Debbie   Come on, you just said so –

Jack (*giggles*)   No, don't . . .

Debbie   It's not too . . .

Jack (*giggles*)   Mammy . . .

Debbie   I can't hear you.

Jack (*giggles*)   Mammy, please . . .

Debbie   Is that too tight, sir?

Jack (*giggles*)   Don't . . .

Debbie   Is that too tight for you?

Jack (*giggles*)   Don't tickle . . .

Debbie (*giggles*)   Is that too tight?

Jack (*giggles*)   Please, Mammy . . .

Debbie (*giggles*)   Is that too tight?

Jack (*giggles*)   Stop it, please!

Both laughing.

Pause.

Debbie   Go on now, there's a good girl.

Pause.

You don't want to disappoint Mrs Stephens.

Pause.

Kimberly.

Pause.

You don't want to upset your father now, do you?

Pause.

Well?

Pause.

You don't want to upset anyone.

Pause.

Kimberly.

Pause.

Kimberly, please . . .

Jack   But Daddy said.

Debbie   I don't care what Daddy said.

Jack But –

Debbie It's only a silly umbrella, now, come on – the early bird catches what?

Jack I know.

Debbie You're late enough as it is.

Jack Sorry.

Debbie What?

Jack I didn't . . .

Debbie What?

Jack I didn't mean . . .

Debbie You've spilt your Coco Pops all down your chin, look.

Jack Oh.

Debbie Dirty so-and-so, what are you?

Jack But I . . .

Debbie Dirty so-and-so. – Here, let me clean you . . .

Jack I didn't mean to wake you.

Debbie What?

Jack I couldn't sleep, I couldn't . . .

Debbie Now, daughter . . .

Jack They were coming for me, Mammy.

Debbie Now, just . . .

Jack Daddy told me.

Debbie He . . . ?

Jack They were going to swallow me whole. They were tapping at the window, Mammy, he promised.

Debbie They're just nightmares.

Jack I know, but –

Debbie   Nightmares, that's all, you were having nightmares.

Jack   But Daddy . . .

Debbie   Daddy nothing.

Jack   Daddy said . . .

Debbie   There's no one coming for you.

Jack   Daddy said I should . . .

Debbie   There's nothing, you hear?

Jack   I should . . .

Debbie   You're going to be late, now . . .

Jack   But I . . .

Debbie   We're running late, come on . . .

Jack   He said I shouldn't bother you.

Debbie   Well, Daddy says a lot of things.

Jack   He told me about the boy . . .

Debbie   Who?

Jack   The golden-haired boy.

Debbie   Look . . .

Jack   He told me the story . . .

Debbie   Daddy doesn't know any boys.

Jack   But . . .

Debbie   Daddy hates boys, you know that.

Jack   In the story . . .

Debbie   He hates boys and little girls.

Jack   On the cloud . . .

Debbie   He's full of hate, Kimberly – Now come on, let's not bicker.

Jack   But . . .

Debbie   I'm your mother, look at me.

Jack   I only meant . . .

Debbie   Take sides with him.

Jack   But . . .

Debbie   After all we've been through . . .

Jack   Please . . .

Debbie   I'm your mother, Kimberly, look at me!

Long pause.

What else did he tell you?

Pause.

What did he tell you about me?

Pause.

You know it's wrong to take sides against your mammy.

Pause.

Kimberly.

Pause.

It's a dreadful sin, you know that, don't you?

Pause.

Kimberly . . .

Jack   Turn it down, for Christ's sake.

Debbie   You know you shouldn't listen to that man.

Jack   Go to sleep.

Debbie   You know you shouldn't forget . . .

Jack   Debbie, please . . .

Debbie   I can't forget.

Jack Just . . .

Debbie What you've done to her . . .

Jack What?

Debbie To us. What you've done to us, you murdering cunt!

Long pause.

'Animal Crackers'.

Pause.

'Bargain Hunt'.

Pause.

'Animal Crackers'.

Jack Debbie, please . . .

Debbie Groucho, Harpo and Chico.

Jack You know she can't sleep . . .

Debbie 'Animal Crackers'.

Jack Look . . .

Debbie I've seen this one before, Jack.

Jack She can't sleep with that noise.

Debbie I remember now.

Jack Turn it . . .

Debbie You remember, don't you, Jack?

Pause.

Jack Debbie . . .

Debbie I remember, look.

Long pause.

Jack Should I go to see if she's all right?

Pause.

Debbie.

Pause.

She's got school in a few hours.

Pause.

She's got school.

Pause.

Should I go and see her?

Pause.

Should I go and tuck her in?

Pause.

I'd like that.

Pause.

I could tell her a bedtime story, couldn't I, Debbie?

Pause.

I could do that.

Pause.

I can hear her.

Pause.

Debbie.

Pause.

Tell me you can hear her.

Pause.

Debbie, please.

Pause.

Come with me.

Long pause.

Come with me, we can take the car. We can see if she's still out there . . .

Debbie   . . . with the sun beating down.

Jack   Debbie . . .

Debbie   You remember, don't you, Jack?

Jack   Look at me . . .

Debbie   And at such . . .

Jack   You've called the school, I hope.

Pause.

You called the school at least.

Pause.

You called the school.

Long pause.

Are you going to just fucking sit there?!

Long pause.

Debbie   And at such a young age.

Jack   Please . . .

Debbie   Hidden in the bushes, with the sun beating down.

Jack   Debbie . . .

Debbie   You remember, Jack. The two of us.

Long pause.

As before, she sings the chorus of 'La Isla Bonita'.

Pause.

*She and **Jack** sing the middle eight/bridge – beginning 'I want to be . . . ' – of 'La Isla Bonita'.*

Long pause.

Debbie   There's someone out there.

Pause.

There's someone out there, Jack.

Pause.

There's some *thing* out there.

Long pause.

She has her breakfast.

Pause.

She turns the corner, I switch on the news. Of course, there was no news, not at that time, not on the terrestrial channel.

Jack   You're late.

Debbie   She's late and she crosses the street to the shelter.

Pause.

There's no one there. Her friends, her jealous friends, they . . .

Jack   They forget.

Debbie   She's too good for them, she's too good – even the doctor said so. The doctor said nothing when he saw her grades, and so she waits. She waits with the rain – the sun – with the sun pouring down – The sun's pouring down and the days are getting shorter, she waits.

Pause.

Jack   There's nothing . . .

Debbie   There's no one around for miles, they forget – They all forget and she's out there all alone. She's out there under the shelter, her umbrella in her bag. The sun's pouring down, but she won't . . .

Pause.

She's a good girl.

Pause.

She's a good girl and they know it. They know it, the bastards. The bastards, the three of them. The three of them watching from the bushes, they can see her now, the monsters, the dirty monsters. They're creeping out under the bushes and they don't take their eyes off her, poor girl.

Jack Poor girl.

Debbie Poor misshapen girl.

Jack Right.

Debbie Poor angel with the three. They see her under the shelter and they creep up the path behind her. Whispering. Whispering in her ear.

Jack Groucho, Harpo and Chico.

Debbie They take her away.

Pause.

They take her out the shelter, they lead her up the hill. They fill her pockets with sweets and lead her up the hill. Huddled up and holding hands, they take her up up over and then they pass the school – Pass the school, past the gate and she says, she says . . . 'But Mammy said,' she says, and they laugh, and the first one says something funny out the corner and now they laugh, they're all laughing. They're laughing so hard and the quiet one honks his horn, and she's raised up on his back and it's horses, playing horses. Clippity-clop clippity-clop, all the while honking – past the school, past the shops, and down behind the houses. 'School? What school? Didn't your daddy tell you? Didn't your mammy say?' – with the rain, with the sun, with the sun blistering their cheeks. They laugh and they gallop and there's no one else for miles.

Jack You lose an hour.

Debbie You lose an hour, and they take her back inside. Inside their room with no doors, the room has no doors.

Jack A window?

Debbie No window. Just a shelf with a towel and they place her on the floor. The dark one lights his cigar, while the others dry her off. They take her bag and her umbrella and she says . . . 'But Mammy said,' she says, and all the time

they're laughing – all the time they're laughing – Place her on
the floor, cross-legged, and dry her down before the rain. They
fight amongst her clothes, and the quiet one takes his scissors,
the small one feeds her peanuts, while the dark one blows thick
smoke. No doors, no windows, and there's no one else for miles.
They're pointing with the scissors, and laughing, snip snip snip.

Pause.

They're laughing, snip snip snip.

Jack   Monsters.

Debbie   Filthy monsters.

Pause.

That's right.

Pause.

That's right, the dirty devils, and they're wading in her blood,
they're wading in our angel and she's drowning in their dirt.
And they're whispering in their ears, and the ticking of the
clock. Past the school, past the houses and they're knocking
down the doors. They're smashing through the windows, and
they're pulling up the floors. They're ripping all the signs down
and sweeping up the tills. The school bell from the school bell
and the shelter from the stop. The bus spins up and over, and
the driver's way ahead, through the windshield . . . Through
the windshield and the channels all dead. 'All dead,' cry the
others, they're screaming now, they're screaming. The blood
the flood and the mothers clinging to the trees. 'But Mammy
said,' they scream, with the ticking down the hour, and the sun
for miles ahead. 'Jesus, save us,' goes the cry. 'Jesus wept for
all mankind.' But the devils lose their patience and they're
snipping at the tongues, they're snipping at the holes. They're
snipping at the doctors, the drivers, the blondes, they're snipping
at her soul – her poor misshapen soul. They're snipping at the
schoolyard, and they're packing up the clothes. Her blonde
hair burns like bonfire, and the breasts all turn and wilt. The
grades dry up in season, and prescriptions turn to ghosts.
Channel-hopping, the floor they're mopping, laughing and

twisting and spinning to the grave – 'Jesus save us,' they're praying. 'Jesus stay!'

Pause.

Jack   And sure enough . . .

Pause.

And sure enough . . .

Debbie   A boy.

Jack   That's right.

Debbie   A golden-haired boy.

Pause.

That's right, on the hour. On the back of a cloud.

Jack   Seated.

Debbie   Seated on the back of a dark distant cloud.

Long pause.

I told you to take your umbrella.

Pause.

What did I say?

Jack   The rain.

Debbie   The weather forecast's rain.

Jack   There's a / good girl.

Debbie   A good girl.

Pause.

The rain washes everything away.

Long pause.

I switch on the news, she turns the corner.

Long pause.

She turns the corner.

Jack   Turn it off now, go to sleep.

Debbie   I told you to take your umbrella.

Jack   Put your head down.

Pause.

Go to sleep, go on.

Pause.

We've got to be up early.

Pause.

Well?

Pause.

What do we say?

Pause.

The early bird catches what?

Pause.

The early bird catches what?

Blackout.

Methuen Drama Modern Plays

include work by

Edward Albee
Jean Anouilh
John Arden
Margaretta D'Arcy
Peter Barnes
Sebastian Barry
Brendan Behan
Dermot Bolger
Edward Bond
Bertolt Brecht
Howard Brenton
Anthony Burgess
Simon Burke
Jim Cartwright
Caryl Churchill
Noël Coward
Lucinda Coxon
Sarah Daniels
Nick Darke
Nick Dear
Shelagh Delaney
David Edgar
David Eldridge
Dario Fo
Michael Frayn
John Godber
Paul Godfrey
David Greig
John Guare
Peter Handke
David Harrower
Jonathan Harvey
Iain Heggie
Declan Hughes
Terry Johnson
Sarah Kane
Charlotte Keatley
Barrie Keeffe
Howard Korder

Robert Lepage
Doug Lucie
Martin McDonagh
John McGrath
Terrence McNally
David Mamet
Patrick Marber
Arthur Miller
Mtwa, Ngema & Simon
Tom Murphy
Phyllis Nagy
Peter Nichols
Sean O'Brien
Joseph O'Connor
Joe Orton
Louise Page
Joe Penhall
Luigi Pirandello
Stephen Poliakoff
Franca Rame
Mark Ravenhill
Philip Ridley
Reginald Rose
Willy Russell
Jean-Paul Sartre
Sam Shepard
Wole Soyinka
Shelagh Stephenson
Peter Straughan
C. P. Taylor
Theatre de Complicite
Theatre Workshop
Sue Townsend
Judy Upton
Timberlake Wertenbaker
Roy Williams
Snoo Wilson
Victoria Wood

Methuen Drama Contemporary Dramatists
include

John Arden (two volumes)
Arden & D'Arcy
Peter Barnes (three volumes)
Sebastian Barry
Dermot Bolger
Edward Bond (six volumes)
Howard Brenton
  (two volumes)
Richard Cameron
Jim Cartwright
Caryl Churchill (two volumes)
Sarah Daniels (two volumes)
Nick Darke
David Edgar (three volumes)
Ben Elton
Dario Fo (two volumes)
Michael Frayn (three volumes)
David Greig
John Godber (two volumes)
Paul Godfrey
John Guare
Lee Hall (two volumes)
Peter Handke
Jonathan Harvey
  (two volumes)
Declan Hughes
Terry Johnson (two volumes)
Sarah Kane
Barrie Keefe
Bernard-Marie Koltès
David Lan
Bryony Lavery
Deborah Levy
Doug Lucie

David Mamet (four volumes)
Martin McDonagh
Duncan McLean
Anthony Minghella
  (two volumes)
Tom Murphy (four volumes)
Phyllis Nagy
Anthony Neilsen
Philip Osment
Louise Page
Stewart Parker (two volumes)
Joe Penhall
Stephen Poliakoff
  (three volumes)
David Rabe
Mark Ravenhill
Christina Reid
Philip Ridley
Willy Russell
Eric-Emmanuel Schmitt
Ntozake Shange
Sam Shepard (two volumes)
Shelagh Stephenson
Wole Soyinka (two volumes)
David Storey (three volumes)
Sue Townsend
Judy Upton
Michel Vinaver
  (two volumes)
Arnold Wesker (two volumes)
Michael Wilcox
Roy Williams
Snoo Wilson (two volumes)
David Wood (two volumes)
Victoria Wood

Methuen Drama Student Editions

Jean Anouilh	*Antigone*
John Arden	*Serjeant Musgrave's Dance*
Alan Ayckbourn	*Confusions*
Aphra Behn	*The Rover*
Edward Bond	*Lear*
Bertolt Brecht	*The Caucasian Chalk Circle*
	Life of Galileo
	Mother Courage and her Children
	The Resistible Rise of Arturo Ui
	The Threepenny Opera
Anton Chekhov	*The Cherry Orchard*
	The Seagull
	Three Sisters
	Uncle Vanya
Caryl Churchill	*Serious Money*
	Top Girls
Shelagh Delaney	*A Taste of Honey*
Euripides	*Medea*
	Elektra
Dario Fo	*Accidental Death of an Anarchist*
Michael Frayn	*Copenhagen*
John Galsworthy	*Strife*
Nikolai Gogol	*The Government Inspector*
Robert Holman	*Across Oka*
Henrik Ibsen	*A Doll's House*
	Hedda Gabler
Charlotte Keatley	*My Mother Said I Never Should*
Bernard Kops	*Dreams of Anne Frank*
Federico García Lorca	*Blood Wedding*
	The House of Bernarda Alba
	(bilingual edition)
David Mamet	*Glengarry Glen Ross*
	Oleanna
Luigi Pirandello	*Six Characters in Search of an Author*
Mark Ravenhill	*Shopping and F***ing*
Willy Russell	*Blood Brothers*
Wole Soyinka	*Death and the King's Horseman*
J. M. Synge	*The Playboy of the Western World*
Oscar Wilde	*The Importance of Being Earnest*
Tennessee Williams	*A Streetcar Named Desire*
	The Glass Menagerie
Timberlake Wertenbaker	*Our Country's Good*